Contents

What is a bee?

A bee is a type of **insect**.
Insects have wings and six legs.

There are many types of bee.

Honeybees visit flowers to collect their
sweet **nectar** and **pollen**. They use the
nectar to make honey.

⇨ This big furry bee is
a bumblebee. It sucks
nectar from a flower.

Egg to Bee

Camilla de la Bédoyère

QED
QED Publishing

Copyright © QED Publishing 2011

First published in the UK in 2011 by
QED Publishing
A Quarto Group company
226 City Road
London EC1V 2TT

www.qed-publishing.co.uk

A catalogue record for this book is available
from the British Library.

ISBN 978 1 84835 585 9

Printed in China

Editor Alexandra Koken
Designer and Picture Researcher Melissa Alaverdy

Words in **bold** are explained in the Glossary on page 22.

Picture credits
Alamy 10-11 Martin Gabriels, 11 David Wooton

Corbis 16 Fritz Rauschenbach

FLPA 5 S&D&K Maslowski, 6t Gary K Smith, 8t, 10b Ingo Arndt/Minden Pictures, 14 , 15t, 15c Heidi and Hans Juergen Koch

Getty 7, 23 Heidi and Hans Juergen Koch, 14 Ingo Arndt

Nature PL 1 Mark Bowler, 4b Georgette Douwma, 6b, 13 Kim Taylor, 18 Jason Smalley, 19y, 19b John B Free

Photolibrary front cover imagebroker, 7 CHASSENET CHASSENET, 8 Konrad Wothe, 9b David M Dennis, 12 Peter Arnold, 16-17 Fritz Rauschenbach, 17t Ritterbach Ritterbach, 20-21 Juniors Bildarchiv, 24 Stefan Ernst

Shutterstock back cover amlet, 2, 24 Markov, 2r Evgeniy Ayupov, 3t Miagli, 5t yxm2008, 20b Kirsanov , 21r studio37

Bees are important insects. They help plants to grow seeds and fruit.

⇧ This is a sweat bee. Not all bees have yellow stripes.

wing

mouth

tail

leg

⇧ This is a female honeybee. She has a sting at the end of her tail.

The story of a bee

Many bees live together in one home. Their home is called a hive.

There is one **queen bee** in a hive. She lays eggs. When an egg hatches a **larva** comes out.

A larva grows into an adult bee. It is called a **pupa** during this stage.

2

larva

1

egg

⇧ Soon, each egg will grow into a larva.

⇧ A bee's egg is tiny. It is about 1 millimetre long.

The story of how an egg grows into an adult bee is called a **life cycle**.

pupa

⇧ A pupa grows wings and legs.

adult

⇨ An adult bee looks very different to a larva.

In the hive

Many thousands of bees can live in one hive.

The queen lays all the eggs in a hive. She can lay thousands of eggs in her lifetime.

Most bees in a hive are **worker bees**. They are all females. Worker bees look after the hive and the eggs, and collect food.

worker bee

queen

⇧ A queen can live for four or five years.

Worker bees build honeycomb inside the hive. It is made of wax and it is full of holes, called cells. This is where the eggs and honey are stored.

Drones are male bees. They have fatter bodies than worker bees.

cell

drone

⇧ Some of the drones will mate with the queen.

⇧ Each cell will be filled with either honey or an egg.

9

Laying the eggs

In spring, the queen bee **mates** with drones. The drones **fertilize** her eggs.

The worker bees have built wax cells for the eggs. The queen bee lays each egg in a cell.

⇨ The queen makes a special glue. She sticks the egg inside its cell.

egg

queen

⇧ Most cells have just one egg inside them.

Three days later, each egg hatches into a tiny white larva.

The queen bee can lay hundreds of eggs every day.

cell

⇨ Each wax cell has a hexagon shape. It has six sides.

larva

Growing and eating

The worker bees feed the larvae with pollen and nectar. The larvae grow bigger. Soon, they are ready to change into adult bees.

The larvae are still inside their wax cells. After feeding, the workers put a cap on top of every cell to close it.

⇦ The workers make sure every larva has enough food.

closed cell

12

Inside each closed cell, the larva changes into an adult bee. A bee is called a pupa while it makes this change.

⇧ As the pupa grows, it looks more like a bee.

13

A bee appears

Ten days later, an adult bee comes out of the wax cell. It looks different from the larva.

Each bee has six legs, and four wings. It has large eyes and a hairy body.

Worker bees have stings, but drones do not.

⇨ The bee eats away the cap on its cell so it can climb out.

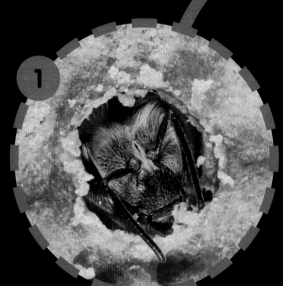

⇧ The bee has large eyes to find flowers.

14

⇐ There are two long feelers on the bee's head.

⇩ A honeybee has yellow and black stripes on its body.

3

4

Busy bees

Most of the new bees are worker bees. They have busy lives.

Worker bees collect pollen and nectar from flowers. Yellow pollen is collected in **pollen baskets**. The bees take it back to the hive.

pollen basket

⇧ A worker bee has pollen baskets on its legs. When the bee visits a flower the baskets fill up with pollen.

⇨ Bees have a strong tongue. They use it to suck nectar from flowers.

Worker bees use the nectar to make honey in the honeycomb.

⇨ In the hive, worker bees are busy cleaning and feeding the larvae.

How bees live

Some bees live in the wild.
Other bees live in special hives.

Wild bees build nests in trees, roofs or walls of buildings.

⇨ A group of bees is called a colony.

Beekeepers build hives for their bees. They collect the honey and the wax that the bees have made.

honeycomb

beekeeper

⇦ Beekeepers wear special suits so that the bees cannot sting them.

18

hive

⇧ Beekeepers take
honeycomb from the hive.
It is full of sweet honey.

We eat the honey. We use
beeswax in make-up, food,
candles and shoe polish.

A new queen

A hive may become too small for all
the bees that live in it.

When this happens, it is time to make a new
hive. The queen bee leads the bees out of
the old hive. They fly to a new place
to build a new hive.

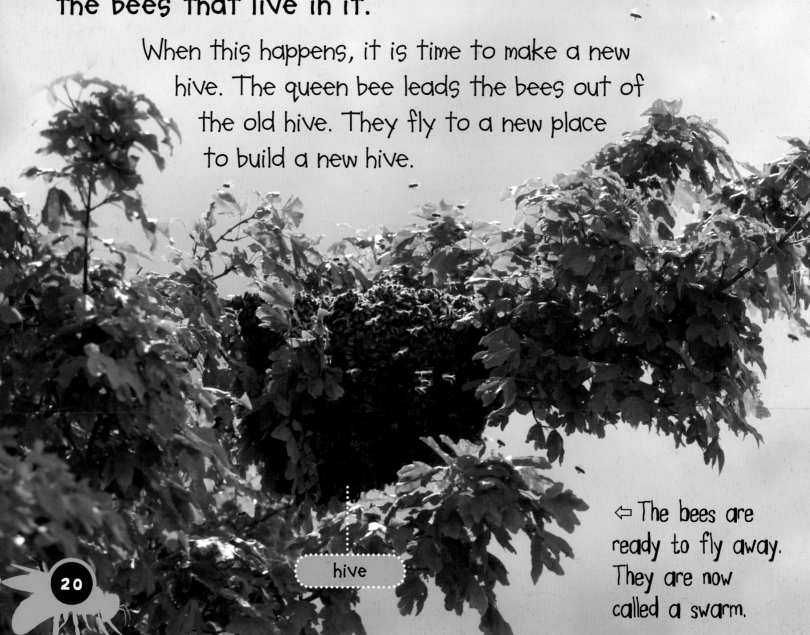

hive

⇦ The bees are
ready to fly away.
They are now
called a swarm.

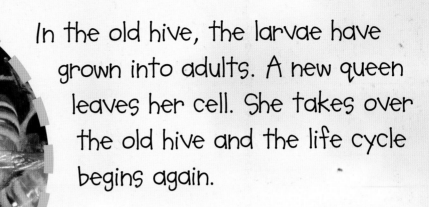

1

In the old hive, the larvae have grown into adults. A new queen leaves her cell. She takes over the old hive and the life cycle begins again.

⇦ A queen's cell is bigger than the other cells.

2

⇨ The queen climbs out of her cell. The workers will clean her.

Glossary

Drone
A male bee.

Fertilize
When a drone fertilizes a queen's egg, it can grow into a new living thing.

Insect
A small animal with wings and six legs.

Larva
An insect's young is called a larva. If there are more than one young, they are called larvae.

Life cycle
The story of how a living thing changes from birth to death, and has young.

Mate
When a male animal fertilizes a female animal's egg or eggs.

Nectar
A sugary liquid made by flowers.

Pollen
A yellow powder made by flowers.

Pollen basket
This is a special place on a bee's legs that is very hairy, and used for carrying pollen.

Pupa
When a larva is changing into an adult it is called a pupa.

Queen bee
The leader of a hive.

Worker bee
Female bees that do most of the work in a hive.

Index

Notes for parents and teachers

 Look through the book and talk about the pictures. Read the captions and ask questions about the things in the photographs that have not been mentioned in the text.

 Watch honeybees at work as they collect pollen and nectar. Can you find where they fly to? Buy some honey together, and use it to prepare or cook food. Help the child to draw a large picture of a bee and show them how to label some of the body parts.

 Use the Internet* or books to research bumblebees. These solitary bees build nests. You could build, or buy, a nest to encourage bumblebees to live in the garden. Find out how to make a bumblebee nest by researching online.

*The publishers cannot accept responsibility for information, links, or any other content of Internet sites, or third-party websites.

 Teach children how to stay safe while investigating animals and their life cycles. They need to learn to keep calm around stinging animals, and to avoid disturbing them. Teach children that they should not touch an animal's habitat. The best way to observe wildlife is to sit still, be patient and quiet – and watch!

 Talking about a child's family helps them to link the processes of reproduction and growth to their own circumstances. Drawing simple family trees, showing them photographs of themselves as babies and talking to grandparents are all fun ways to engage young children.